Matt Hasselbeck

by Michael Sandler

Consultant: Norries Wilson
Head Football Coach, Columbia University

New York, New York

Credits

Cover, © Joe Murphy/WireImage; Title Page, © AP Images/Ted S. Warren; 4, © Jonathan Ferrey/Getty Images; 5, © Tom Hauck/Getty Images; 6, © Jim Bryant/EPA/Corbis; 7, © Kevin Casey/WireImage/Newscom; 8, © Lane Turner/Boston Globe/Landov; 9, © Ronald C. Modra/Sports Imagery/Getty Images; 11, © Jonathan Wiggs/Boston Globe/Landov; 12, © Corbis; 13, © Rick Stewart/Getty Images; 14, © AP Images/Paul Sakuma; 15, © AP Images/Michael Conroy; 16, © Steve Ringman/The Seattle Times; 17, © Steve Ringman/The Seattle Times; 18, © Courtesy of Convio; 19, © White House/Reuters/Landov; 20, © Frank Polich/Reuters/Landov; 21, © Larry French/Getty Images; 22, © AP Images/Ted S. Warren; 22Logo, © KRT/Newscom.

Publisher: Kenn Goin
Senior Editor: Lisa Wiseman
Creative Director: Spencer Brinker
Photo Researcher: Omni-Photo Communications, Inc.
Design: Dawn Beard Creative

Library of Congress Cataloging-in-Publication Data

Sandler, Michael, 1965-
  Matt Hasselbeck / by Michael Sandler ; consultant, Norries Wilson.
      p. cm. — (Football heroes making a difference)
  Includes bibliographical references and index.
  ISBN-13: 978-1-59716-773-4 (library binding)
  ISBN-10: 1-59716-773-8 (library binding)
  1. Hasselbeck, Matt—Juvenile literature. 2. Football players—United States—Biography—Juvenile literature. 3. Football players—United States—Conduct of life—Juvenile literature. I. Wilson, Norries. II. Title.

  GV939.H3356S26 2009
  796.33092—dc22
  [B]
                                    2008041110

For more information, write to Bearport Publishing Company, Inc., 45 West 21st Street, Suite 3B New York, New York 10010. Printed in the United States of America in North Mankato, Minnesota.

10 9 8 7 6 5 4 3

CONTENTS

Waiting for a Win

The city of Seattle had waited 21 long years for the Seahawks to win a playoff game. Was the wait almost over?

On January 14, 2006, Seattle held a seven-point lead against the Washington Redskins. With five minutes left in the game, however, Washington could still make a comeback.

Seattle needed a **first down** or the Redskins would have a chance to tie the game. The Seahawks' coach, Mike Holmgren, called the play—a pass for quarterback Matt Hasselbeck. Would Matt come through and end Seattle's long wait?

Seahawks fans before the game on January 14, 2006

Matt Hasselbeck

The Seahawks hadn't won a playoff game since December 1984.

Sweet Victory

Just before the **snap**, Matt looked at Washington's **defenders**. They were lining up to **blitz** from the left. If Matt threw a pass, they would flatten him!

Ignoring his coach's call, Matt changed the play. He told **fullback** Mack Strong to run right, then handed him the football. Mack rarely carried the ball, but Matt's last-second decision worked like magic. Mack burst free for 32 yards (29 m).

The first down produced a Seattle field goal and an unbeatable 10-point lead. Thanks to Matt, the long wait would soon be over!

Mack Strong (#38) runs with the ball for a 32-yard (29-m) gain.

Mack (#38) and Matt celebrate their team's 20-10 win.

Mack's 32-yard (29-m) run was the longest of his career.

Football Family

It takes lots of experience to ignore a coach's call. Luckily, Matt had plenty of it. He grew up in a family of football players. His mother, Betsy, had seven brothers, and six of them were high school quarterbacks. His father, Don, played in the National Football League (NFL) for nine years.

Don spent hours teaching Matt and his two other sons the game. He even coached the boys' football teams.

Since Don played for many different teams, the family moved around from city to city. After Don **retired**, the Hasselbecks settled in Norfolk, Massachusetts. There Matt became the quarterback at Xaverian Brothers High School.

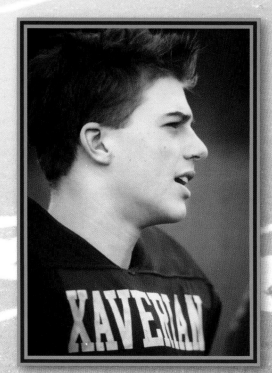

Matt in his
Xaverian uniform

Matt's younger brother Tim went on to play in the NFL from 2001 to 2007. His other brother, Nathanael, played football for Boston College.

Don Hasselbeck (#85) played tight end for the New England Patriots, the Los Angeles Raiders, the Minnesota Vikings, and the New York Giants.

Trouble and Travel

After finishing high school in 1993, Matt went to Boston College (BC). He wanted to become a **starter** for their football team—the Eagles. He imagined himself becoming a star.

Things didn't go that smoothly for Matt, however. He argued with his coaches. They kept him on the bench. He sat around feeling sorry for himself, thinking: *Why am I not playing?*

Then, in his junior year, Matt took a trip with a group of students to Jamaica during spring break. They were going to spend a week teaching **orphans** and working with **leprosy** victims. The trip would change his life.

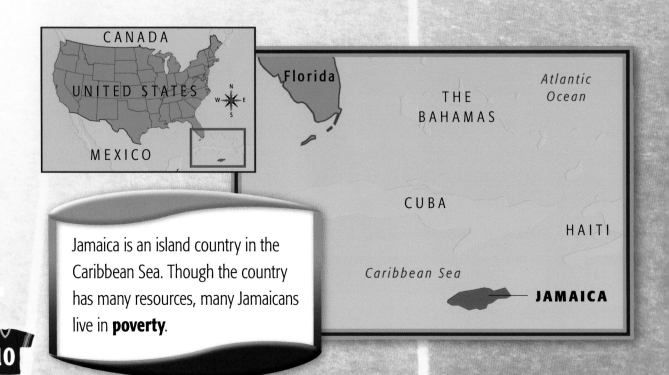

Jamaica is an island country in the Caribbean Sea. Though the country has many resources, many Jamaicans live in **poverty**.

Matt during football
practice at BC

A Different Person

Matt was shocked by what he saw in Jamaica. People lived in shacks without electricity or running water. School kids studied beside piles of garbage crawling with rats.

"It hit me over the head with a hammer to wake up—you don't have it that bad," Matt said. "It just really changed me."

Matt was different when he returned to BC. He stopped feeling sorry for himself. Instead of complaining, he worked as hard as he could. Soon, his hustle, intelligence, and talent earned him the starting job on the BC team.

A town in Jamaica similar to the one Matt visited

Matt runs with the ball during a game against the University of Pittsburgh Panthers.

At Boston College, Matt threw for over 4,500 yards (4,115 m) and 22 touchdowns.

13

Seahawks to the Super Bowl

In 1998, after college, Matt was drafted by the Green Bay Packers. The team already had a star quarterback, Brett Favre, so Matt barely played. Then, in 2001, Matt was **traded** to Seattle.

Matt became the Seahawks' starting quarterback and helped the team improve. Beginning in 2003, Seattle made the playoffs three years in a row. Then, the big win over the Redskins in 2006 sent Seattle into the **NFC Championship Game**. There, Matt led the Seahawks to a 34-14 victory over the Carolina Panthers. Seattle **advanced** to its very first Super Bowl.

Brett Favre

Matt breaks away from Pittsburgh Steeler James Farrior for an 18-yard (16-m) gain during Super Bowl XL (40).

In Super Bowl XL (40), Seattle faced the Pittsburgh Steelers. Matt played well, completing 9 of his first 11 passes. However, Pittsburgh won the game, 21-10.

Making a Difference

Even as a Super Bowl quarterback, Matt has never stopped thinking about his life-changing Jamaica trip. He also hasn't stopped trying to make a difference in the lives of others.

One way he does this is through his work with the Matthew Hasselbeck **Foundation**. This group raises money for many programs in Seattle that help less fortunate children. He also sponsors a quarterback and receiver camp. This allows high school students to work on their passing and catching skills. The money raised by the camp goes to different **charities**.

Matt gives instructions to a young player during quarterback camp.

Matt advises young athletes during quarterback camp.

Matt also appears on posters and in videos encouraging people to wear seat belts while driving in cars. In addition, he raises money to help find a cure for cancer.

Supporting Soldiers

Matt also helps soldiers and their families. He appreciates the **sacrifices** these men and women make when they leave home to go **overseas** to fight. He knows how much their kids miss them. After all, his own father was often away from home when he was growing up.

One way that Matt reaches out to these heroes is by spending time with injured soldiers. He visits hospitals where they are being treated and talks with the soldiers to cheer them up. It's great "if I can lift their spirits for a while," he says.

He also works hard to keep these soldiers close to their families. In 2007, his foundation gave $10,000 to Fisher House. This group pays for families to stay in housing that's right next to the hospitals where their loved ones are patients.

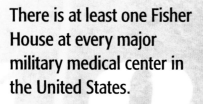

There is at least one Fisher House at every major military medical center in the United States.

A family, at the Fisher House in Washington, D.C., visits with President and Mrs. Bush.

Matt also goes to military bases to show his support for the troops. He signs autographs and often plays football with the soldiers.

Helping Each Other

Often, when Matt helps others, he finds he's helping himself as well. For one big playoff game against the Green Bay Packers in 2004, Matt rented a **luxury box** for kids from the **Make-A-Wish Foundation**. These seriously ill children were thrilled to be at the game.

The game was exciting, but Matt threw an **interception** that cost Seattle the win. Afterward, feeling glum, he went up to see the kids. "It put everything in perspective, real quick," Matt said. The kids were still so excited to see him that he couldn't be upset for long. As a football hero, Matt realizes that helping others is more important than playing the game—and it's even more rewarding.

Matt throws the pass that was intercepted by the Green Bay Packers.

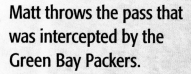

Matt during a game in 2008

In the 2007–2008 season, Matt led the Seahawks to the playoffs for the fifth straight year.

The Matt File

Matt is a football hero on and off the field. Here are some highlights.

 Matt's football coaches at Boston College didn't want him to go to Jamaica. They were worried he might get sick—which he did. Matt ended up in the hospital and lost over 20 pounds (9 kg). Even so, he was happy he had made the trip.

 Don Hasselbeck didn't let his sons play organized football until he was around to coach them. He was worried that other coaches might teach them to play the wrong way.

 Matt keeps getting better and better. In 2007, he set career highs for both passing yards and touchdowns.

 During his career, Matt has made the NFC Pro Bowl team three times.

 What is Matt's favorite sports memory? Super Bowl XVIII (18). Matt—then in third grade—got to watch his dad make the play that helped the Los Angeles Raiders win the game.

Glossary

advanced (ad-VANSST) moved on

blitz (BLITS) a defensive play where more players than usual run at the quarterback; it gives the quarterback very little time to throw

charities (CHA-ruh-teez) groups that raise money or run programs for people in need of help

defenders (di-FEND-urz) players who have the job of stopping the other team from scoring

first down (FURST DOWN) the first play in a series of four football plays; a team earns a new first down by gaining 10 yards (9 m) or more

foundation (foun-DAY-shuhn) an organization that supports or gives money to worthwhile causes

fullback (FUL-bak) a player whose job is to block defenders, keeping them out of the way of running backs; this player may also run with the ball

interception (*in*-tur-SEP-shuhn) a pass that is caught by a player on the defensive team

leprosy (LEP-ruh-see) a disease that attacks a person's skin, nerves, and muscles

luxury box (LUHG-zhuh-ree BOKS) a special group of seats in a stadium that has great views of the field

Make-A-Wish Foundation (MAKE-UH-WISH foun-DAY-shuhn) a group that tries to provide children suffering from serious diseases with special experiences

NFC Championship Game (EN EFF SEE CHAM-pee-uhn-*ship* GAME) a playoff game that decides which National Football Conference (NFC) team will go to the Super Bowl

orphans (OR-fuhns) children whose parents have died

overseas (oh-vur-*SEEZ*) across the ocean

poverty (POV-ur-tee) being very poor

retired (ri-TYE-urd) stopped working, usually because of age

sacrifices (SAK-ruh-*fisse*-iz) things people give up for important reasons

snap (SNAP) when the center passes the ball to the quarterback to begin a football play

starter (START-ur) a person who plays at the start of a game; the best player at a position

traded (TRADE-id) exchanged for a player on another team

Bibliography

Attner, Paul. "Turning Out the Slights." *Sporting News* (January 20, 2006).

Bishop, Greg. "Seahawk Hopes Words Won't Haunt Him Again." *New York Times* (January 7, 2008).

Tomase, John. "Hasselbeck on Mission: College Trip Buoys QB." *Boston Herald* (February 2, 2006).

Read More

Gilbert, Sarah. *The History of the Seattle Seahawks.* Mankato, MN: Creative Education (2005).

Kelley, K. C. *NFC West: The Arizona Cardinals, the St. Louis Rams, the San Francisco 49ers, the Seattle Seahawks.* Mankato, MN: Child's World (2008).

Stewart, Mark. *Seattle Seahawks (Team Spirit).* Chicago Norwood House Press (2008).

Learn More Online

To learn more about Matt, the Matthew Hasselbeck Foundation, and the Seattle Seahawks, visit **www.bearportpublishing.com/FootballHeroes**

Index